HOW 1 PEANUT BUTTER & JELLY SANDWICH

15 Steps

to accomplishing
just about anything
in business & life

J. E. Edwards

How to Make a Peanut Butter & Jelly Sandwich
15 Steps to accomplishing just about anything in business & life

by J. E. Edwards

Illustrations by Becky Brown

Available in Paperback at . . .
Amazon & Other Online Retailers
Bookstores

Also Available as a Kindle eBook

Library of Congress Control Number: 2018907089

ISBN-13: 978-1-7323342-0-5

facebook.com/authorjeedwards

DEDICATION

To my "darling daughter" Megan

You changed my life . . .
in ways I could have never imagined.

You are one of my greatest gifts!

May you find success and happiness
with "Your"
Peanut Butter & Jelly Sandwich "Story".

CONTENTS

ACKNOWLEDGMENTS

This book came about, because of an exercise in junior high that inspired me so much, that it has always stayed with me.

I would like to thank the teachers in my past, for their thoughts and ideas that helped me. I didn't recognize it at the time, but I now realize years later, that they contributed more than they will ever know and brought me to this point of writing my book. Teachers make a difference!

To my grandparents, Alfred and Sarah Nelson, who taught me kindness, giving, and that the simple things in life, DO matter.

To my cousin, Linda, who taught me, it's never too late.

To my family and friends who taught me many lessons in life. Some of the lessons took a while to learn, some I just recently learned, and for those I haven't learned yet, I am forever grateful.

Thanks to Becky Brown for her illustrations. She captured the feel of the book perfectly! Becky's favorite peanut butter & jelly sandwich is chunky peanut butter & raspberry preserves on wheat toast!

A big thank you to my spouse Laurel, for her love, support and all the time and energy spent editing and helping to lay this all out, because that is definitely not my strong suit! Laurel's favorite peanut butter & jelly sandwich is creamy peanut butter & grape jam on white!

I also want to thank Susan Seidl for her editing expertise and words of encouragement! If Susan were ordering a peanut butter & jelly sandwich, she would say . . . "Hold the peanut butter"!

1
How It Began

"Everything is as easy
as making a peanut butter & jelly
sandwich, if you just put things
in the right order."

J. E. Edwards

When I was in junior high, I had a class called "Liberal Arts". In this class, we did an exercise that is still with me today.

Now I sit and wonder after all of this time - why it has stayed with me, but my thoughts of it throughout the years are always with an important lesson.

It made an indelible impression and I have come to believe that this simple exercise is the answer to every project, problem or situation that needs to be thought through, with a successful outcome.

I wanted to share this knowledge with others, but when I sat down to begin this, I wasn't sure if I was writing a self-help, or business book. I realized it truly falls into multiple categories. It's a book that will help anyone organize steps for completing a goal - so this book is for everyone!

Did you ever pick up a self-help book, start to read it and immediately think to yourself, this is too difficult or complicated to understand? Did it make your head spin?

As you read this book, you may think to yourself, this is too simple and reads like a children's book. Maybe so, but I'm asking you to put on your "kid hat" and open your mind! Even if you are the CEO of a major company, I'm telling you that things do not have to be complex to get something out of them. Simple can be better!

It can be the most simple ideas that bring us the biggest breakthroughs.

Why do we read an endless number of self-help books, spend lots of money and try so many things to become successful at whatever we are trying to accomplish? We try to visualize and meditate our way to the top. Sometimes we even try to copy successful people. "If it worked for them, it will work for me!" That can sometimes help, but it's not you - not yours.

What if I told you that by following a simple exercise you could organize steps to successfully achieve anything, propelling you to a success as you have never known?

This simple exercise that I am speaking of, teaches how important it is to identify clear & precise steps for successfully achieving any goal.

What you need to do is stand up and get busy!

2
Let's Get Started

"The way to get started is to quit talking
and begin doing."

Walt Disney

Do you sometimes feel overwhelmed by a project
or a decision? Do you sometimes not know where to
begin? Maybe you are even putting off starting it.
I'm sure everyone has felt that at one time or another.

Enough, Enough, ENOUGH!

You could read all of the business and self-help
books in the world, but if you don't get out of your
chair, map your steps and get moving, then it will not
happen.

I can't say this Enough!

Action alone isn't enough. Have you seen some
people running around in a frenzy most of the time?
They have the energy, desire and ambition, but they
don't have direction. Those people are always
looking for that perfect answer to it all and are "busy
getting things done", but not getting any closer to
their goal, because they continue to get off track.

You need steps to get there!

Some think that multi-tasking their way to success is the answer. They "busy" themselves right past success many times. They don't even have time for a peanut butter & jelly sandwich! They miss out on all the important things in life!

I'm sure that there will be some exercises that I ask you to do that will seem silly or unimportant, but I'm asking you to trust me. The smallest things can bring great insight when you have completed each of them.

Remember this is a process and you must do it "Step-by-Step".

When you break something down into its simplest form, that's when you can also find the most basic solutions. It's also when you can have your greatest achievements, because you have taken the task and mapped out one step at a time.

This formula is in every success story you have ever heard! What? Yes! It is in every success story you have heard! What I mean by that is, in every success story, someone has taken steps to achieve their goal. They may not have done 15 Steps, but they took steps.

Now, I'm going to show you how to create your own list of 15 Steps to make YOUR success happen!

First, identify what goal you want to accomplish. Is it to improve a current situation in your life? To create something new at work? To be debt free? To start a new business?

Whatever it is that you want to accomplish, you can do it in 15 Steps if you have the drive to stick with it!

This book will show you how to compare the steps of reaching your goal to the making of a sandwich.

Your goal will be your sandwich!

So sit back, open your mind and have fun with what I am about to teach you. Are you ready for the journey?

You could make a peanut butter and jelly sandwich for the trip ...

3
Making The Wrong Sandwich

"Your time is limited, so don't waste it
living someone else's life."

Steve Jobs

I want to get something very important out of the way first . . .

If you start off making the wrong sandwich, there is definitely nowhere to go from that point! It sounds funny doesn't it? But people do it all the time, all over the world. You even know people right this moment, whether it's a family member or a friend, who is eating the wrong sandwich!

That is like putting raspberry jelly on your sandwich when you hate raspberry jelly!

We make decisions everyday based on our likes, values and beliefs, but when it comes to the big goals in life, we can make the wrong sandwich!

Let's picture for a moment that you like the basic peanut butter & jelly sandwich on white bread, with smooth peanut butter & grape jelly. There is absolutely nothing wrong with that sandwich. That sandwich is who you are and it doesn't matter who else likes or dislikes it!

Let's say, for example, you decide that you are going to use prickly pear cactus jelly on your sandwich, not because you like it, but because other successful people have done it and it also sounds really cool!

The big problem is, that you come to find out that you hate prickly pear cactus jelly! Now it may be great for others, but it's not for you.

A lot of times we think we want to accomplish a goal, but sometimes it is for all the wrong reasons. Don't spend your time and effort on something that is not 100% what you want to do.

The #1 thing
you must do above all else -

Create goals that will truly make you

HAPPY!

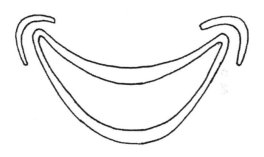

I want you to take a few moments and really think about what I just said and not just breeze over it.

We make goals, because we think we want something. We may have grown up believing that this was what we wished for, but maybe it was someone else's dream that we believed would make us happy.

Who are you? What would you want in life, if you could have anything you wanted? If you could only do one thing for the rest of your life, regardless of money, position, where you lived, etc., what would it be? What kind of person do you want to be?

Setting goals is what life is about, but if you set the wrong goals, you will never have true happiness. That's like making a sandwich that you don't like and yet you continue to make and eat it, over and over! Why would you do that?

It doesn't always have to be a huge goal, maybe you just want to build a patio. But, for larger personal, career, or relationship goals, you must be very clear on what you want.

How do we make certain we are not making the wrong sandwich? Ask yourself these questions - What makes you feel good? What makes you truly happy in life?

Make a list of all of the things that make you feel good. It could be things that you like to do, places you like to go, people you enjoy being around, etc.

Tap into you, and you will find your goals! What do I mean by that? If you like certain things, why would you not do more of those things? If you like to do a certain hobby, then could you turn that hobby into a business?

Create goals from the things you like in life and watch how things change!

You will be making the RIGHT sandwich!

4
Your Goal

"I don't wait for moods.
You accomplish nothing if you do that.
Your mind must know
it has got to get down to work."
Pearl S. Buck

Identify Your Goal

Get some paper and on the first page, write the goal you want to accomplish.

Find a quiet place with your paper, where you can brainstorm without any interruptions. I want you to set a timer for 90 minutes of totally uninterrupted time!

Brainstorm and write down every thought you have on what you want to accomplish.

This is a dreaming session . . .

Now for Your Foundation . . .

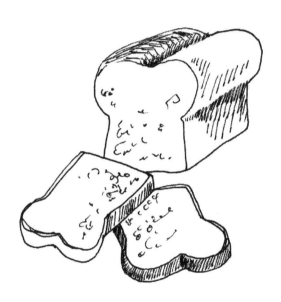

5
Basic Foundation Exercise

"If you can dream it, you can do it."

Walt Disney

I want you to be patient and do something out of the ordinary. This is your basic foundation exercise. Just as a house sits on a foundation to make it stand, you need to have a foundation for your life and the things you want to accomplish. Without a foundation nothing will stand or endure.

Don't cheat, this is the whole point of foundation work and this exercise and if you cheat and don't do what I ask, then you will only be cheating yourself!

If you are not willing to do things one step at a time, then all may fail. This is one of the moments in your life that will determine your future. Are you ready?

Here we go - set this book down and . . .

Get a sheet of paper. Draw a horizontal line across the middle of the page, so that you have two equal areas - a top and a bottom section.

On the top section of your paper write:

My goal will be
MY "Peanut Butter & Jelly Sandwich"
and I am ready to make it now!

My "Peanut Butter & Jelly Sandwich" is

_____

(Write the goal that you want to accomplish)

– –

On the bottom section - write:

My 5 Reasons Why
I Want to Accomplish This Goal!

1 _____

2 _____

3 _____

4 _____

5 _____

The 5 reasons are very important for you to identify. There are always reasons that drive us. Some are very basic and others are very deep and personal.

You may think that you don't have 5 reasons, but I'm asking you to take the time and put thought into identifying 5. Really think about it! When you must come up with 5 reasons, it forces you to really tap into your feelings and uncover what your motivations are for wanting this goal.

If you don't have good reasons to do it, then you are less likely to stick with it! If you can't come up with 5 good reasons, maybe that goal is not right for you. Maybe it's the wrong sandwich!

Don't move on until you have written down 5 reasons and no less!

Every time you create a new goal - repeat this exercise.

You must know why you want to do what you want to do.

The important thing is to identify why you want to do what you are setting out to accomplish. Maybe one of the reasons is financial independence for your family. Or another reason is simply to prove to yourself or someone else that you can do it! You must understand why you want things, then they become more important to you. You own them!

What we do in life must have meaning, or purpose. If there is a purpose, then you fulfill yourself and ultimately other people in your life.

Hang the paper up where you can see it - EVERYDAY!

Place it above your desk, in an area where you work, or on the bathroom mirror, just so that you see it in the morning and a number of times throughout your day. Make extra copies to post it in multiple locations if you like.

Read it in the morning when you get up and before you go to bed at night. Read it every day until you attain your goal.

You must do this step! As with everything, this alone will not make it happen, but this is your important foundation.

Now that you have your foundation, are you ready for the next step?

Here we go –

You must do all of this work and
remember, no cheating!

Set this book down and go get ‑

> 1 loaf of bread
> 1 jar of peanut butter
> 1 jar of jelly
> 2 butter knives
> 1 plate

If you don't have each of these items, then take
the time to get them. You must have enough
ambition to get in the car, walk, or hop on your bike
to go get them. If you don't have enough energy to
do this, then how are you going to accomplish your
goal?

You need to do this easy part or you will not be
ready for the rest. Remember, if you want to change
your life, you will need to have enough ambition to
do this! Come back when you have all of the
ingredients.

. . . are you ready now?

let's start . . .

FIRST

Make Your Own Set of Steps

Sit down and write out "Step-by-Step"
How to Make a
Peanut Butter & Jelly Sandwich.

IMPORTANT!

Do not move ahead
until you have done this!

NEXT

Make Your Sandwich Following Your Directions EXACTLY –

Word for Word as Written!

Read the directions out loud, a few words at a time, as you do what the directions say to do – "Step by Step"!

Pretend you don't know anything about how to make a peanut butter & jelly sandwich, as if you have never even seen a sandwich before and ONLY do what your directions tell you to do – literally.

Imagine you are standing in front of a group of people and you are reading technical directions on how to put something together. This can be fun and just think, you get to eat what you make!

NO ADDING STEPS!

Don't read any further until you have made your sandwich.

GO DO IT . . .

WELCOME BACK!

- What happened in this exercise?

- How accurate were your directions?

- Did you miss any important steps?

- Were your directions unclear?

- What could you have done differently?

- How many steps were actually missing?

Did you put peanut butter on your hand because you were not clear with your directions? That's funny, but not when you are trying to reach an important goal!

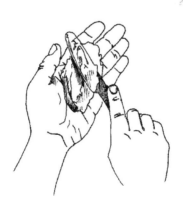

LAST

Enjoy Your Creation!

Have your sandwich and eat it too!
Enjoy what you have built!

Just like making a peanut butter & jelly sandwich and eating it, you must have fun along the way and bring joy into everything you do.

Remember when you were a kid and even making a sandwich was fun?

This exercise has shown you how important it is to write out clear, precise steps needed to successfully accomplish a goal and then to complete each of those steps exactly, just like making a peanut butter & jelly sandwich.

Are you good at writing out clear directions and steps?

If you don't do each step needed in the right order, who knows what you'll end up with, or you may not even reach your goal! When we miss steps we need to take to accomplish whatever we want to do, then we are unsuccessful.

Could these be the simple things that have kept you from reaching your goals?

Another very important lesson is to have fun doing whatever you are attempting to accomplish - things that make you happy!

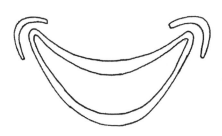

Let's go back to what I had told you previously . . .

It Takes

15 Steps

to accomplish
just about anything you want!

and . . .

It really does take 15 Steps
to make a
Peanut Butter & Jelly Sandwich!

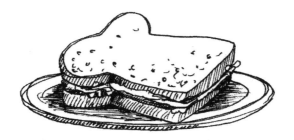

6
MAKING A
PEANUT BUTTER & JELLY
SANDWICH

"It is a happy talent to know
how to play."

Ralph Waldo Emerson

For anyone who wants to get something done,
writing down the steps required to accomplish it, is
the first thing to do.

I know that 15 Steps, in some instances, may
seem like too many or too few, but believe it or not, it
really does take 15 Steps to make a peanut butter &
jelly sandwich!

Seem impossible?
Let's try it together!

The 15 Steps to Making a Peanut Butter & Jelly Sandwich . . .

 1

Lay out all items needed for the project on a table -

> 1 loaf of bread
> 1 jar of peanut butter
> 1 jar of jelly
> 2 butter knives
> 1 plate

2

Remove the twist tie or clip from the bread bag, take out two slices of bread from the bag and place them side-by-side on the plate.

 3

Take the jar of peanut butter in one hand and with the other hand, open the jar and then set the jar of peanut butter and lid down onto the table.

 4

Take the jar of jelly in one hand and with the other hand, open the jar and then set the jar of jelly and lid down onto the table.

5

Grasp one butter knife by the handle in your dominant hand.

 6

Dip the other end of the butter knife into the jar of peanut butter, making sure to get approximately one tablespoon of peanut butter on the knife.

 7

Pull the knife out of the jar of peanut butter and evenly spread the peanut butter that's on the knife onto the top side of one slice of bread, covering it to the edges.

8

Redo steps 6 and 7 until the one side of that slice of bread has been evenly covered with the amount of peanut butter that you would like.

 9

Scrape the excess peanut butter on the knife back into the jar of peanut butter by drawing it across the top of the jar edge and when all peanut butter is off of the end of the knife, then lay the knife down.

 10

Grasp the clean unused butter knife by the handle in your dominant hand and dip the other end into the jar of jelly, getting as much jelly on the knife as you can.

11

Pull the knife out of the jar of jelly and evenly spread the jelly that's on the knife onto the top side of the other slice of bread, covering it to the edges.

 12

Redo steps 10 and 11 until the one side of that slice of bread has been covered with the amount of jelly that you would like and lay down the knife just used.

 13

Place one slice of bread on top of the other, so that the sides with the peanut butter and jelly are together.

14

Grasp one of the butter knives previously used, by the handle in your dominate hand. Now, cut the sandwich evenly in half and set the knife down onto the table.

 15

Enjoy your sandwich!

Did you notice that Step 15 is to

"ENJOY"

what you have accomplished?

Now . . .

Are you ready to see how the 15 Step Process can work for whatever you want to accomplish?

In making a peanut butter & jelly sandwich, Step 1, is to "Lay out all items needed for the project on a table".

It may seem too simple, but if you systemically work on one step at a time, you will reach your goal.

Take a moment to clear your head and get ready! Did that make you hungry? I would make a peanut butter & jelly sandwich before starting this next section, to take along for the trip of your lifetime!

Identify Your 15 Steps

I want you to start your mind working! Even if initially you think you have no ideas as to how to accomplish your goal, I know you have ideas - whether the ideas are right or wrong at this point in time.

Identifying what you think you need to do and how you think you need to do it, is the first step to successfully achieving any goal. This is more about brainstorming and getting your mind to focus on what you want, not on having all of the answers. You are training your mind to put down thoughts and ideas. You must do this for it to work.

I want you to write down everything that you can think of that you will need to do, to accomplish what you want!

I know this can be difficult and you may not have all of the information needed to be able to do this exercise, but that is not the important thing at this point. Training your mind to brainstorm, to dream and to formulate your thoughts may take some time.

This is a very important step to accomplish!

This will be your first draft, so don't worry if you feel you don't have all or some of the information you need.

Now is the time to start your research! Research everything about the goal you want to accomplish. Go online and search for information. Reach out to others who have accomplished the same goal. Talk to professionals, family and friends who can help. Research until you believe you have all of the things listed that you will need to accomplish your goal.

This may take a few days, or it may take you weeks. But, you must gather all of the information, thoughts and ideas to get you where you want to go.

If it's a more simple goal, like getting out of debt or building a deck on your house, then it may only take you a few days to gather your information. If it's a large goal of starting a business, it could take you a month or more.

Take a piece of paper and down the left side, write Step 1, Step 2 and so on, to Step 15, leaving some space between each step for writing. If this is a large goal, then you may need a separate page for each step.

Next to Step 1, simply write the word "Brainstorming". This represents the thoughts and ideas that you have compiled.

Next to Step 15, write the word "Enjoy"! You must enjoy your goal, or remember - what's the point?

Since Step 1 is "Brainstorming" and Step 15 is "Enjoy!", that leaves you with 13 remaining steps that YOU will be creating.

Fill In YOUR Steps

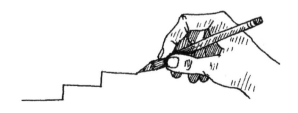

Now, you will begin digging through all of your brainstorming, research, interviews, etc. It might help to circle or highlight important items as you go through.

Write in your steps in the order in which they will need to be completed.

Identify Step 2, then 3 and so on, until you have filled in each number, through Step 14. That will complete your 15 Steps!

This is YOUR
Peanut Butter & Jelly Sandwich
"Goal"
which will become your Peanut
Butter & Jelly Sandwich
"Story"
when you accomplish it!

If a small goal, you may think that 15 Steps sounds like too many, but you need to really think it through and break it down into 15 small steps.

If a large goal, you may think there are a lot more steps than 15, but trust the process and narrow it down to 15!

Your steps may each have a lot of items, but none the less, you must make it 15 Steps.

If you are starting a business and one of the steps is marketing and advertising, you might think there should be many more multiple steps, so for example, put all of the ideas for marketing and advertising into one step. This step will be the initial set-up, but throughout the life of the business, you will continue to come back to it.

It will be a large step with lots of information, but then you can break things down into manageable items within that step that you can check off. When all of the manageable items are completed, then that entire step will be done.

This is not an easy exercise!
I totally understand,
but nothing worth accomplishing
is easy!

1 Brainstorming

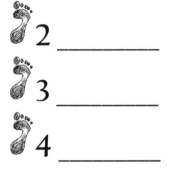

2 _____

3 _____

4 _____

... through Step 14

15 Enjoy!

Remember . . .

starting down the road
is the hardest part.

Please find quiet times, so that you can think through the steps. These steps may take hours, days or even weeks to put together. Take your time.

You may not be able to do this on your own. If that is the case, then search out help until you can get this exercise completed and you feel that your 15 Steps are a good road map for what you need to do.

When you have completed this exercise, then you will be able to work on each step, one at a time. Each step must have your total focus and when that step is completed, then move on to the next step.

You could make a BIG poster or use a dry erase board with a list of your steps on it and when you have completed each step, you could check it off. Seeing progress will be satisfying and rewarding!

If I were you, I would make a peanut butter & jelly sandwich for this exercise and have fun. Feed your brain! You could even draw pictures on the side of your poster for inspiration, while you eat your sandwich!

Remember when you were back in grade school and it was fun creating projects with markers? I hope you haven't forgotten to have fun, have you? Even in the hardest of times, you can find enjoyment along the way. If you can do that, then you will be surprised at how much more energy and spirit you will have to get you where you are going and you will enjoy life to its fullest!

Whether you are a student, teacher, parent, blue or white collar worker, stay-at-home mom or dad, or the CEO of a company, creating these 15 Steps is the first vital step to anyone's success!

Imagine if for everything in your life you wanted to achieve, you wrote out 15 Steps with a picture next to it. What if it was a new car? What if it was a very expensive car that you thought you could never own? Write out your 15 Steps on how to buy that car. Hang up the steps with a picture of the car, so that you can look at it every day!

Continue your steps while you picture seeing that car sitting in your driveway . . . how it would make you feel behind the wheel!

Maybe one of your steps is to get an extra job for a period of time. It doesn't matter, as long as you write out your steps and START working on them. You can do it!

Remember - you need to write your steps out as detailed as possible, so that you can achieve success!

Set this book down and get to work!

You CAN do it!

7
Your 15 Steps

"You'll be on your way up!
You'll be seeing great sights!
You'll join the high fliers
who soar to high heights."

Dr. Seuss

Whew! How you feeling now? I'm sure you may be feeling positive and overwhelmed! The hardest part of any trip is getting started and you have accomplished that!

I know this is not easy,
but as you continue through this book,
you are one step closer to
reaching your goal!

No matter the goal, whether it is large or small, complex or simple, it can be broken down into 15 Steps.

Now let's go through the steps of making a peanut butter & jelly sandwich and how to relate them to your steps.

Since I don't know what your goal or project is, I

need to compare this to something. Let's use the goal of starting a business.

If your goal is something different, then your steps will be different. But, whatever it is that you want to accomplish, it can be done in 15 Steps.

Example:
Steps to "Starting a Business"

PB & J Step 1: Lay out all items needed . . .

YOUR Step 1: Brainstorm!

PB & J Step 2: . . . take out two slices of bread and place them side-by-side on the plate.

YOUR Step 2: Place the brainstorming piece of paper and a new piece of paper side-by-side. Write out your steps.

PB & J Step 3: Take the jar of peanut butter in one hand . . .

YOUR Step 3: Create your business plan. Just like the bread for your sandwich, this is the foundation of everything you are trying to do.

List what is unique about your company idea, market

analysis of the competition, demographics you need to target, product line or service, company structure, etc.

There are many resources available to create a business plan. Within your business plan, you may have additional steps, but the plan itself is one step.

PB & J Step 4: Take the jar of jelly in one hand . . .

YOUR Step 4: Get assistance and training. This is the sweet part, just like jelly - where you will learn from the experts! You will need business assistance and training for the things you don't know.

PB & J Step 5: Grasp one butter knife . . .

YOUR Step 5: Business Formation. What kind of set up will you have? Whether an LLC, S Corp or Sole Proprietorship - choose whatever works best for you. Set up the appropriate accounting, bookkeeping and tax records. Hire an accountant or do it yourself. Set up your bank accounts, accounting policies and processes, and insurance protection. Where do you want to locate your business? Is it an online or brick and mortar store? A good start-up lawyer could prove to be very important.

PB & J Step 6: Dip the other end of the butter knife into the jar of peanut butter . . .

YOUR Step 6: This is where you "Dip" into the gooey stuff of it all. How will you build the product or set up the service you are going to market? Who are your customers? What does the product or service do that improves your customer's life? What is the price you need to charge for the product or service to be profitable?

How will you manufacture or produce the product? Will you sell direct, or through distributors? Who is going to sell it? How will it be delivered? This is the who, what, where, when and how of your business.

PB & J Step 7: Pull the knife out of the jar of peanut butter and evenly spread the peanut butter . . .

YOUR Step 7: This is where you "spread" the entire branding idea of your business. In 15 words or less, what is your business? The brand is your peanut butter and that makes everything possible! What is the personality of the business?

PB & J Step 8: Redo steps 6 and 7 until the one side of that slice of bread has been evenly covered . . .

YOUR Step 8: Review your accounting policies and decisions and determination on how to build your product or set up your service. Is anything missing, or is there something you can add? This is YOUR business. This could also be another step and not a review, that's up to you.

PB & J Step 9: . . . then lay the knife down.

YOUR Step 9: Lay it all down - total up how much money you will need to start your business and begin operation. If a brick and mortar store, some items will be different than an online store or service company. This will be another area you need to brainstorm and research. Don't forget to budget for that lunch bag to carry your peanut butter & jelly sandwich to work every day!

PB & J Step 10: . . . dip the other end into the jar of jelly, getting as much jelly on the knife as you can.

YOUR Step 10: Another "sweet" spot of getting you to your goal! Create an online presence. Whether your business is an online, brick and mortar, or service company, you still need a website and an online presence. This is critically important with more and more purchasing happening online.

Who will create the website? Who will create and maintain your social media? Who will handle your advertising?

PB & J Step 11: . . . evenly spread the jelly that's on the knife onto the top side of the other slice of bread, covering it to the edges.

YOUR Step 11: Here is where you spread your jelly to the world by promoting your business with marketing and advertising.

PB & J Step 12: Redo steps 10 and 11 . . .

YOUR Step 12: Review how much money you need and make additional tweaks to your online presence. You can't review or revisit these things enough throughout the life of your business. Again, this could be another step instead of a review.

Whatever you think you will need for money - add 40% to that amount. That is my "sticky" piece of advice.

PB & J Step 13: Place one slice of bread on top of the other . . .

YOUR Step 13: Here is where it all comes together. Get financed! Determine whether you are applying for a bank, or SBA loan, crowd sourcing, personal investment or explaining your peanut butter & jelly sandwich idea to your family and friends for any help they may provide.

PB & J Step 14: . . . cut the sandwich evenly in half and set the knife down onto the table.

YOUR Step 14: It is not enough to do all of your steps, you must continue to grow your business. This step will continue for the life of the business.

If you are not starting a business, this step will look different. Perhaps you want to accomplish something personal, such as going back to school, so maybe this step is your graduation, but you still want to continue to grow through learning, right?

Show everyone your sandwich - reach out to other companies, bloggers, etc. and ask for some promotion in exchange for product sample or service. Continue to look for ways to market and advertise. There's lots of ideas that help one continue to grow!

Even if you are successful at this point, you don't just stop. It wouldn't make much sense to climb half way up a mountain and stop. Do you want to make it to the top? Even if you make it to the top, there will be others below that are climbing as well - your competition! At that point you'd better be looking for a higher mountain!

PB & J Step 15: Enjoy your sandwich!

YOUR Step 15: This is YOUR Peanut Butter & Jelly "Goal" that has become your "Story"! This is enjoying the sandwich of your labor. If you don't take the time to enjoy your peanut butter & jelly sandwich, then what is the point? Plus, this will energize you for your next goal!

I know what you're going to say - that this example of starting a business is too simple. Yes it is simple, but I don't have any idea what your goal is that you want to attain and even if it is starting a business, there are a lot of things that may be different, depending on what type of business you want to start.

What I just showed you is an illustration of 15 Steps in a very basic sense and your steps will likely be in a different order and much more detailed. This was simply to demonstrate how this plan works.

My whole point is to teach you the 15 Step Process and that it will work, no matter what you want to accomplish!

Whether you are starting a business, are a high school student who wants to attend a good college or a CEO wanting to grow a specific division of a company - whatever your goal is, you can accomplish it in 15 steps!

Whether a simple or complex goal, put it into 15 Steps. It will challenge you to take a complex goal and simplify it, or a simple goal and create more details to accomplish it successfully!

In addition, adding steps to any goal makes it easier to achieve, one step at a time!

8
For The Group

"If you can laugh together,
you can work together"
Robert Orben

If you really want to have some fun, do this with a group of friends, family members, organization members, co-workers, management team, church members, students, or any other group you can think of, that could benefit from learning to accomplish goals successfully. That would be everyone!

This exercise in almost any group setting, creates team building and teaches how important it is to identify and be very detailed and clear with directions to accomplish any goal successfully, "Step-by-Step".

First think about what you learned doing this individually . . .

To accomplish your goals, you need to be very clear about identifying each and every step and then complete those steps in the right order.

Also important - while you set out to achieve just about anything, have fun along the way! If you can't have fun getting to where you are going, then what's the point?

Life should be a fun journey! The most successful people in life enjoy themselves and have fun as they work hard every day.

Let's get started with this fun group
exercise . . .

First, choose a group leader.

He or she does not have to be the actual leader of a group (boss, senior person, highest rank, etc.), it can be whoever you want it to be.

If you are choosing someone other than yourself, then you will need to share all of this with them.

It would be so much more fun to surprise the entire group - why don't you be the leader? It is great practice being a leader!

This Section Is For the Group Leader

Your objective is to lead the group through this exercise.

Hopefully, no one in the group knows what this is about, so everyone can be surprised. You do NOT want anyone prepping ahead of time, so don't announce the topic of this meeting!

Give the meeting a fun name that does not give away what you are up to - how about "Team Building Snack Session"?

When inviting your group, be sure to ask if any have nut allergies. If so, ask them to let you know in advance, so you can discuss options. They may still want to attend, but just not eat their sandwich. Swear them to secrecy, so the fun isn't spoiled.

If a workplace group, make the meeting right before lunch, or middle of the afternoon and they can eat what they create! Think of all the fun you can have!

Your time limit will determine how many people you want to invite to this group. You will need to decide that ahead of time.

Allow approximately 15 minutes per person, so they can write out directions, you can make their sandwiches and have time to talk about the outcomes and the lesson. A good size group would be 6 to 8 people.

I personally think, the more people the better! I understand in a work setting, that time is very important, but the value you will get out of this exercise is very vital.

You could have multiple groups at different times, but you will need to have the group members promise not to share the topic of the meeting and what happens, before they leave their session.

If you are doing this as a workplace exercise, it doesn't matter if it is an entry level person or the CEO, everyone can learn from writing out complete and accurate directions!

What fun for the group to have everyone on the same level learning together!

You will need to prepare
with the following:

1 or 2 loaves of bread
1 jar of peanut butter
1 jar of jelly
2 butter knives
paper plates
napkins
1 pack of wet wipes, if no water nearby
1 roll of paper towels - for cleaning
1 pen for each person
1 sheet of paper for each person

Select an area with a table large enough for all of the people to sit around and room for you to work at one end, or use a separate "work table".

Leading the Exercise

1.

Hand out a piece of paper and a pen to each person in the group.

2.

Inform the group that each person needs to write out "Step-by-Step" directions on how to make a peanut butter & jelly sandwich and put their name at the top of the paper.

3.

Tell them they cannot talk to one another until everyone is done and has turned in their directions to you.

4.

After everyone has turned in their directions, take one plate and one set of directions from the group:

Do NOT read the person's name on the set of directions.

Start reading the directions on the piece of paper out loud - a few words at a time, while you are making the sandwich from the directions they gave to you, "Step-by-Step".

IMPORTANT - Follow the directions
<u>EXACTLY</u> –
WORD FOR WORD AS WRITTEN!

Pretend you don't know anything about how to make a peanut butter & jelly sandwich, as if you have never even seen a sandwich before and ONLY do what the directions tell you to do - <u>literally</u>!

When you have read all of the directions on the piece of paper, you are finished with the sandwich.

This is the teaching part of the exercise. What fun! Are they telling you to put peanut butter on one side on the bread, but they haven't told you to take it out of the bag yet? What a funny mess!

You want this to be fun and entertaining, so that they understand the entire point of this exercise - that your goal must have clear and accurate "Step-by-Step" directions to successfully arrive at any outcome that you set out to achieve.

5.

Take the plate with the sandwich, walk to the person who wrote those directions and set it in front of them, explaining that this isn't to embarrass anyone, but to teach an important lesson.

6.

Choose the next participant's directions and repeat until you have gone through everyone's directions.

When you have completed everyone's sandwich, invite them to eat their creations while you go around the room and have everyone answer the following two questions –

- What did you learn?

- Can you think of ways that you can utilize what you learned?

9
Ever Read A Recipe Book?

"It's always good to go over the recipe beforehand, so you can easily think of the next thing that needs to be done".

Guy Fieri

Have you ever picked up a recipe book? That doesn't mean that you know how to cook, but just out of curiosity?

In the book, there is recipe after recipe of "Step-by-Step" directions on how to create certain foods.

That sounds familiar doesn't it? Maybe every recipe doesn't have 15 Steps, but nonetheless, there are steps to get you to the end result.

Many people have read the same recipe, did the same steps, but came to a different end result.

Some of us measure and follow directions more accurately, we purchase different product brands and types of ingredients, our oven temperatures vary, the list goes on and on . . .

As I was writing this, I noticed a recipe book sitting on the shelf. In the beginning of that book, there was a page that had notes that outlined helpful tips to assist with cooking.

These were tips that undoubtedly the cook had learned from not so favorable outcomes.

Some of the tips that I noticed were . . . "Chocolate scorches quickly, so never take your eyes off of it while it is melting." "Semisweet and bittersweet chocolates are interchangeable in most instances." "Dark and light brown sugar can be used interchangeably." and "It is always important to pre-heat your oven completely!".

Wow! This really has to do with life! The most important tip is to pre-heat your oven completely. If you don't pre-heat by doing your steps, then the recipe will not turn out exactly as it should.

There also was a section in the beginning of the recipe book titled "Terms That You Should Know". Some of those terms were crush, chop, grate, peel, toss, fold, mix, blend, cool, chill and measuring the right way. Interesting!

I was thinking that all of life can be equated to a recipe book.

To sum it up . . .

Crush your goals

Chop your dream into small parts

Grate your way through

Peel back each layer

Toss some things out & toss some in

Fold in the good with the bad

Mix in happiness

Blend all experiences

Cool and relaxed is always best

Chill out when needed

Measure things carefully & often

Whatever your dream or goal -

the 15 Steps
to completing your goal
is "Your Recipe"!

10
Ingredients

"Success isn't just about what you accomplish in your life, it's about what you inspire others to do."

unknown

There are many ingredients that we each have in our lives that make up who we are. These ingredients are family, friends, hobbies, faith and so much more.

Even the things that you lack in life, shape who you are. They too play an important role in how you have come to be that person, your foundation and who you will continue to become!

Why am I talking about this and why is this important?

I want you to continue to look at who you are. Maybe up to this point in your life, depending upon your age, you may not have had a lot of experiences, but it is never too early or too late to begin to make changes for a better you.

Here Are Your Ingredients ~

Personal Experiences
Economics
Amusement
Nurture
Uniqueness
Thoughtfulness

Beliefs
Units
Troubles
Talent
Encouragement
Resolve

&

Job
Education
Love
Links
Youth

You did notice what the ingredients spell, right? Just checking to see if you were paying attention or eating your sandwich!

Personal Experiences

Let's start with the first ingredient - "Personal Experiences". These are all of the experiences that you have had in your life up to this moment. It shapes who you have become. But the very important part of this is, that it doesn't have to shape who you will be.

Starting today and moving forward, what experiences can you begin to have that would move you closer to that person you want to be?

Economics

What kind of money did you grow up around? This can influence who you are and your attitude toward money. Do you have a limiting view on money, because you grew up in a household of poverty? Or did you grow up with wealth and your view of money is unlimited?

How do you think this influences you today? How can you change negative thoughts? If you grew up in poverty, does that stop you from taking any type of financial risks today? Does it stop you from trying anything new?

Amusement

This is your hobbies, interests - the things you enjoy doing. These things you could have begun as a small child, or maybe you developed new hobbies as an adult.

Interests make us who we are and what brings us happiness. What do you like to do that brings you happiness? Is the interest a break from everyday life?

Have you turned your hobby or interest into your job? Could you turn your hobby or interest into your own business? Is your hobby something that you could share with others to bring them happiness?

Nurture

What kind of nurturing did you receive as a child growing up? Were you encouraged to go after what you wanted? Did you have help achieving things you wanted to do as you grew up? Did you have love and understanding, or criticism?

If you didn't have the nurturing to be successful growing up, what can you do to help yourself today?

Who could you reach out to as a mentor? Seek them out - there are many people who would be honored to mentor and help you along the way. Having courage to ask for help, is sometimes the bravest thing you can do.

Uniqueness

We are each unique in who we are and in everything that makes us who we are. You need to look at all of your strengths (make a list) and see how you can utilize them to achieve what you want.

Thoughtfulness

This category can be many things. It's about donating to charities, volunteering or your everyday care toward others.

If someone needs help, do you jump in? How does that affect your outlook on life? Only when we reach beyond ourselves, do our lives begin to change for the good of all!

Beliefs

A big one! Your belief system encompasses everything from your personal faith, how you view the world, to your morals and values. This is truly what makes you who you are.

How do you view your values? What would you like to improve? Are some beliefs holding you back from achieving greatness? What is your personal faith? You must have a foundation of beliefs. Define them and live them!

Units

This is your family. Family has a huge impact and it's one of the most important areas of our lives, so we need to take time to look at this very closely.

Parents, stepparents, foster parents, spouses, siblings, children and other relatives influence how we view things and determine some of the decisions we make.

Family shaped much of who we are now, as we grew up, for better or worse, and continues to make a difference in our lives as adults.

Does your family have an influence on your life today? Did you not have a family and how has that influenced you?

Are there negative things that you could change? Do you need boundaries for the negative areas?

Can you talk to your family members about how they impact your life? Tell them about how they have influenced you in good ways!

I challenge you to look at your positives and how you can build the life you want. Even negative things in your life have made you who you are today. Maybe you had to do some things on your own, making you a very strong person. Focus on the positives!

Troubles

I think you know what this one is - I really didn't want to bring up negative things, but this is something everyone has had and it has helped to shape your beliefs, ideas and even some of your personality.

You must really think about this area and how you can move forward from any troubles of the past.

Maybe you are going through troubles right now, but it doesn't matter. The past is gone, and even the present will be gone in a few minutes. How you move forward is up to YOU!

Talent

Now this area should be super easy for you. What are your talents? What are you good at that others are not? Can you turn one of your talents into a business or hobby to make extra money?

Do you have a talent that could improve the lives of other people? All of your talents are unique to you and make you who you are. Embrace them!

Encouragement

Are you encouraged by anyone?   Parents, siblings, teachers, spouse, good friend, mentor, co-worker, boss or others you know? If you have someone who encourages you, then your chances of success have increased greatly!

If you don't have someone, then reach out and find a mentor in something that you are interested in!

Maybe there's someone that you look up to and want to be like. Make them your life mentor!

Resolve

The dictionary states that resolve is "marked by firm determination", so this one is totally on you.

Have firm determination day in and day out and you will be surprised at how far you will go!

Job

What is your current way of making a living? Maybe you're too young to have a full time job yet, but that doesn't stop you from dreaming and deciding what you want to do. Dream what you want to be, doing what you like to do, so that it doesn't seem like a job!

Are you happy and content? Are you working for an employer? Do you want to work for yourself?

If you like your job, how can you advance yourself? If you are not happy, then do something different!

Start TODAY thinking of how you can change your current job situation!

Education

Whatever your level of education, this also influences your thinking, income level, and opportunities.

I'm telling you that your mindset, abilities and effort will take you places further than any piece of paper.

Now to do certain things, you do need to get some education, but if you just get a diploma and don't continue to better yourself through on-going education, you will not go far.

Love

Love has many definitions. What does love mean to you? How does love support your life?

Does the love you give or get in your life make you a better person, or hold you back? Do you receive more love than you give?

How can you give more love to others in your life?

Links

These are your friends. Unlike family, we choose the friends in our life. For that reason, friends can sometimes have more of an impact on us than family.

Do your friends bring happiness to you? Do they make you a better person? Do they encourage you? Do they brighten your day by being around them, or do they bring negativity into your life?

Life is about choices and we need to choose wisely to be a better person!

Youth

This is the kid in you! We all have a kid inside us, no matter what age we are. This is the free spirit, innocent and fun-loving person in us all.

We must tap into that person as much as possible, because that is where we dream! Only when you dream and have fun can you see that ALL things are possible!

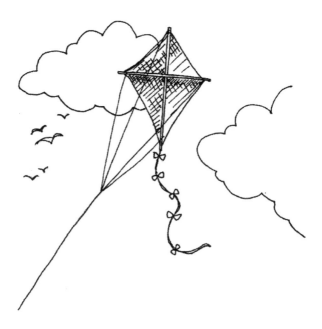

Now it's YOUR Turn . . .

Get multiple sheets of paper for this next exercise. At the top of the first page, write "Personal Experiences". At the top of the second, write Economics and continue to write each of the remaining ingredients listed on page 72, one per page.

Take some time and under each ingredient, write down what it means to you, positive or negative. For some of you, negatives may be hard to think about. But, remember, even the bad and unpleasant things that have happened to us, have shaped who we are.

Every single person has some negatives that have happened to them, even if overall they came from a very good life.

If you write down any negative experiences, how can you change those into positives moving forward? Maybe you came from a family that didn't care about you. Then think about how you could have your own family someday and what you would do differently for your children. Being the best loving parent would sure change a negative to a positive!

If you came from a family with parents who

loved you, think about how you can build upon that for the next generation!

I know it can sometimes be difficult to look at your life, but this is all part of the process to get you where you need to be as a person and toward reaching your goals.

As you worked through these ingredients I asked you many questions. In addition to writing on your piece of paper what each ingredient means to you, answer every question in each of the ingredients. This is meant for you to look very closely at your life and how you can improve upon yourself to be a better person. We all have room for improvement!

Remember, that your Peanut Butter & Jelly Sandwich "Story' is not just about the goals you reach, but also who you are as a person. It is the complete story of you!

Look at each question and honestly answer for yourself. We go through life in a hurry and don't take the time to analyze our lives and think of ways to make them better.

Some questions will be so basic, but they may just be the small light bulb that changes your life!

Set this book down,
do the exercise and
come back when you are done.

OK - since you are back reading again, then you did the exercise right? Let's evaluate this.

Were any of the items negative? How can you get beyond that negativity and move forward in a positive direction?

Remember, no matter what has happened in your past, or is happening in your present, it does NOT have to be what your future looks like!

No matter what your age is right at this moment, you can grow into who you want to be. Do something for me right now, OK?

Take a piece of paper and write out 15 things you want within 5 years, such as values, goals, or basic characteristics. Whether you will be 20 years old or 60 years old, it doesn't matter. It is important to become who you want to be. Even if you think you are successful, a good person, or "on the right track", you can always do more and become better!

Do you want to be self-sufficient, a leader of a group in society, drive a nice car, have a strong faith, be an honor student, have a strong marriage, be a good parent, be a good friend, be a person that other people want to follow, or be compassionate to others through your time and money?

Your background doesn't matter, whether you came from being homeless or from wealth, you can choose to be better and be who others aspire to be.

There is a song written by Lori Mckenna, performed by Tim McGraw called "Humble and Kind", which I think can relate to this book. If you haven't heard the song, please take time to listen to it or read the lyrics.

There are a few lines that sum up what it means to truly succeed. What determines success isn't all about money. It is about being the best possible you and giving back.

It's about what kind of person you should be after attaining your dreams and reaching the success that you've worked so hard for. To feel pride, but to stay humble and kind.

Most importantly, once you get there, to remember to take the time to help others achieve their goals.

You are making your own
Peanut Butter & Jelly Sandwich
"Story"
of your life,
not only with your 15 Steps
to accomplishing your goal,
but with
who you are as a person
and
who you will evolve into.

11
Add-Ons

"Oh, the things you will find,
if you don't stay behind."

Dr. Seuss

Are you ready to tackle your steps one at a time? You can do it! Stay focused every day on each step until you finish that step, check it off and then move on to the next one.

In the meantime, I want to share some other things with you as "food for thought".

There are a lot of different kinds of peanut butter & jelly sandwiches, just as there are different kinds of people, goals, dreams, needs and wants. I have heard that some people even put bananas or pickles on their peanut butter & jelly sandwiches!

Add-ons are things that you do, as you are creating and achieving your goal.

Some add-ons that you could do while achieving your 15 Steps, could be to make time for others through volunteering, belonging to a gym that you go to during the day as a break, or taking a walk in nature while you eat your peanut butter & jelly sandwich.

There are a lot of add-ons that each of us have, that go into creating our own Peanut & Jelly Sandwich "Story" of our life. We choose what kind of peanut butter we like, whether it be smooth or crunchy, what kind of jelly we like, depending on our taste and of course, we can even choose what type of bread we like. That is what makes everyone and their dreams unique and fun.

If you choose to add any extras to your sandwich, there are still only 15 Basic Steps to reaching your goal. If you add any extras, you can incorporate them into whatever steps they may fit into.

If in Step 14 of making your peanut butter & jelly sandwich, you decide to put it into a pan and grill it when you're done putting it together, then that becomes a part of YOUR Step 14!

12
Sticking To The Roof of Your Mouth

"Successful people are simply those with successful habits."

Brian Tracy

What is one thing that almost everyone hates when eating peanut butter? Yes - it is the peanut butter sticking to the roof of your mouth!

As great as peanut butter is, that is an obstacle with eating it. It is so good while you are eating, but then all of a sudden, you realize that there is peanut butter stuck to the roof of your mouth - ugh!

It is the same with life. You are going along conquering your steps to reaching your goal and then peanut butter is sticking to the roof of your mouth, so to speak. Well, not literally peanut butter on the roof of your mouth, but the things life is made of, which can be just as sticky.

You are probably asking, "What does peanut butter on the roof of your mouth have to do with anything?". It refers to the "sticky" problems, people and events that happen to all of us.

Almost daily, things may come up that are challenging, that can sometimes throw us for a loop. Okay, sometimes they can really throw us, so we are hardly able to recover.

However, that is where you must really dig deep, refocus, and concentrate on your steps!

This is why it is vital to have your 15 Steps, so when those times come along, you will not even have to think about how to get yourself back on track.

Working on your 15 Steps day in and day out will become a habit. You will be in the moment of whichever step you are on and will continue to move forward.

13
Be Healthy

"The groundwork of all happiness
is health."

James Leigh Hunt

Now, to another very important part of your Peanut Butter & Jelly Sandwich "Story". You can do everything in this book up to a point, but you must have good health! If you are out every day eating your peanut butter & jelly sandwich, you must keep your body in the best shape possible, so that you can conquer your goal!

Have you thought about putting a sliced apple or banana on your sandwich? How about some flax seeds? What other healthy items could you add to that great sandwich of yours?

Just like tackling your steps to reaching your goal, you need to do steps to keep yourself in good health. Do you have an exercise program?

Use the 15 Step method and create another goal - "Improving Your Health!"

How about a personal health goal to "Eat Good Healthy Food"? Consume less processed and fast foods and more that are organic and natural, while watching your portions and calories. It will help you control your weight while eating all of those peanut butter & jelly sandwiches!

Again, use the 15 Steps for a healthy food program for YOU!

14

Have Fun

"Have fun along the way.
That's what life is about!"

J. E. Edwards

Okay, we have covered a lot in this book so far, but this chapter is as important as all of the rest.

After all, what is the point of focusing all of your time and energy on reaching your goals if you forget to have fun along the way? It is a scientific fact that laughing and smiling improves health! Laughing is easier than exercise and watching how you eat, so why wouldn't you do a lot of it!

Why not have fun with your friends? Invite a group of friends over and put out smooth & crunchy peanut butters, jellies & jams, various breads, honey, bananas, berries & other fruits, various nuts & seeds, raw veggies, chocolate chips, marshmallow fluff, pickles, potato chips, bacon - anything you can think of, to make creative peanut butter & jelly sandwiches. How about peanut butter fondue? What about peanut butter cookies for dessert? Maybe reach out to make a new friend to have fun with!

You could even pack up peanut butter & jelly sandwiches, load up your friends or family and take off on a road trip to new adventures.

When you go to a restaurant, if there is a peanut butter & jelly sandwich on the menu, order it, then give the waiter or waitress an extra $5 or $10 in their tip and tell them why. Life is fun when you pass on some happiness!

An idea to help others, is to buy a few jars of peanut butter & jelly and a few loaves of bread and drop it off at a local pantry, so others can enjoy peanut butter & jelly sandwiches!

All of these things you can do to have fun will also remind you about your steps and goals.

What else can you do to put more fun into your life? Start a new hobby? Go somewhere you haven't been before and experience that new adventure?

Challenge yourself - at least once a week, to do something that is totally fun, new and makes you laugh!

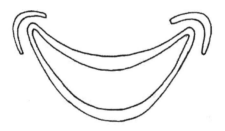

What does it all mean?

The dictionary's definition of success is "The accomplishment of an aim or purpose".

That doesn't mean you have to have a huge goal or dream. You can have your large goals of starting a business, growing a current business or developing a new career. Maybe you need to build a shed, remodel a home or start that garden you always wanted, however, day in and day out we all have smaller things we need to accomplish.

The list can go on and on, but the whole point is, everything that you do in life, is for a specific aim or purpose. You must get into that mindset and then start to accomplish goals in 15 Steps.

You may even have five things going at once, but if in each one of the five things you are working on, you are utilizing the 15 Step Process, then you know how to get there - you have maps. Check off each step as you accomplish it and your motivation will continue to grow!

Wouldn't it be fun to have a number of lists hanging up, checking things off as you go? You might even complete more than one goal at a time!

Fun Tidbits!

I know this is a book about accomplishing your goals, but, it is also a book about fun and peanut butter & jelly sandwiches!

Here are some fun facts about peanut butter & jelly to share with family and friends. You will be knowledgeable, while making your dreams come true!

- The first known reference to a peanut butter & jelly sandwich happened in 1901, when it was mentioned in the Boston Cooking School Magazine of Culinary Science and Domestic Economics, written by Julia Davis Chandler.

- Thomas Welch developed Grapelade from concord grapes in 1918, which proved to be extremely popular as a ration among the troops during World War I. They combined it with their peanut butter ration, to create a delicious tasty treat in the field.

- Peanut butter & jelly were staples in military rations during WWII, and when soldiers arrived home from the war, they popularized the practice of using them on bread. That helped to further boost peanut butter & jelly sales.

- With the invention of packaged sliced bread, in the 1920's, peanut butter & jelly sandwiches skyrocketed in popularity.

- 68% of Americans prefer creamy peanut butter to crunchy in their peanut butter & jelly sandwiches.

- The average American eats over 1,500 peanut butter & jelly sandwiches before they graduate high school.

- 1 in 7 Americans add honey and about 1 in 21 add raisins, marshmallows, butter and bacon to their peanut butter & jelly sandwiches!

- Peanut butter & jelly sandwiches are still considered to be a "comfort food" by 30% of Americans.

- One acre of peanuts will make about 30,000 peanut butter & jelly sandwiches!

- According to a 2016 survey, nearly half of Americans regularly eat peanut butter & jelly sandwiches.

- Most people make a peanut butter & jelly sandwich in about 3 minutes.

- The record for the most peanut butter & jelly sandwiches made in one hour is 49,100 by Temple University's Main Campus Program Board in Philadelphia, PA. On Sept 29, 2016, approximately 1,350 volunteers used 4,500 loaves of bread, 4,280 lbs. of peanut butter & 3,551 lbs. of jellies and preserves, according to The Guinness World Book of Records.

- 53% of Americans surveyed in 2016, said exactly half peanut butter and half jelly is the perfect ratio for a sandwich.

- 96% of people put the peanut butter on first, before the jelly, when making a sandwich.

- Three in ten parents make a peanut butter & jelly sandwich for themselves, while making them for their kids.

- Half of millennials agree - peanut butter & jelly sandwiches are their go-to lunch item.

- 75% of Baby Boomers say that peanut butter & jelly sandwiches remind them of their childhood.

- 10% of Americans are very adventurous, when it comes to their peanut butter & jelly sandwiches and combinations can include things like olives, bologna, American cheese and even sunny side up eggs!

- As for jelly, grape is still the favorite for peanut butter & jelly sandwiches in the U.S., with strawberry jelly coming in at a close second.

- In 2000, Pres. George W. Bush told Oprah his favorite sandwich was peanut butter & jelly and then jumped up and down on her couch!

- According to The Guinness World Book of Records, the largest peanut butter & jelly sandwich weighed 5,440 lbs. and was made by Wild Woody's Chill and Grill, in Roseville, Michigan.

April 2nd is
National Peanut Butter & Jelly Day!

Now you have some trivia that you can impress your friends with while you make peanut butter & jelly sandwiches together!

15
Give

"If you can't feed a hundred people, then feed just one."

Mother Teresa

It is the absolute most important thing in life - to Give!

The best thing in life is making ourselves and others happy by giving! It doesn't matter how successful you become, or how much money you make, but how you give what you have back to others.

No matter your lot in life, everyone has something to give! Giving does not have to mean donating money - you can give of your time and talents in many places if you look. Volunteering can be one of the most rewarding things you can ever do, no matter your age. It may even mean meeting new friends in new places!

Recipe for a Successful Life

1

Make "Your Own" Peanut Butter & Jelly Sandwich "Story".

2

Have fun along the way, creating your own sandwiches, "One Step at a Time".

3

Enjoy "Your" sandwiches and share your "Story" with others!

4

Give back to the world as a result of your success.

Be An Inspiration!

16
What I Think

"Winners are losers who got up and
gave it one more try."

Dennis DeYoung

I have met a number of successful people in my life and I have come to learn that they have two common traits that make them successful. The first is that they map out their steps to get them to where they want to go and the second is that they work at it every day without giving up. It is not about the clothes you wear or anything else, it is about ACTION!

It is about deciding what you want and going after it until you get it! It is not about asking permission, thinking about if you have the qualifications, or anything else. It is about ACTION and going for it!

When I was a sophomore in high school, I wanted a job at a local newspaper. The job was for someone to drive a van around town and drop off bundles of newspapers for the carriers to deliver.

The interview was going great and I thought I had the job, but then suddenly, the interviewer asked

"Will you able to drive a stick shift?" I answered in a blink of an eye - YES!

Well, I got the job, but there was one small challenge - I didn't know how to drive a stick shift, let alone a van. I had only had my driver's license for a couple of months!

I had just four days to learn, but I knew that I could do it! I'm telling you that you must trust in your abilities, even if you don't always know all of the answers.

The interviewer did ask "Will you be "able" to drive a stick shift?" and yes - I knew I would be "able" to drive a stick shift by Monday morning, so it was the truth!

I started looking for someone who owned a stick shift and I learned how to drive one by Monday morning!

As I look back, without even knowing it, I took steps to get that first job, including showing up for my interview and learning how to drive a stick shift. It taught me an important lesson about confidence, actions and completing steps to get me to where I wanted to go. This is what every person that effectively accomplishes anything does.

They may not map out their steps on paper, but they have the steps in their mind. It may seem haphazard in the way they go about it, but believe me, they do have steps.

You can't get somewhere if you don't know where you are going and if you don't know where you are going, you will never get there!

Life is one goal after another! When you finish Step 15 on your goal, then start the next goal, or work on multiple goals at once. You will continually be working on the Peanut Butter & Jelly Sandwich "Story" of your life. It will be a combination of all of your numerous 15 Step stories that will make up your life "Story"!

When you were a kid outside playing and eating peanut butter & jelly sandwiches, you were always ready to play with a friend. When we tap back into our "child state", we can have fun, dream big, help others and accomplish whatever we want.

Remember too as a kid, when you were doing something that you loved to do? You could do it from sun up to sundown every day. Did it seem like you never got tired or bored? Bring that same energy to what you now want to accomplish.

Never lose that kid in you - never grow up too much!

Part of your Peanut Butter & Jelly Sandwich "Story" is your "sweet spot" of happiness. What is your definition of happiness? If it is to be successful, then what parts of success make you happy? Is giving to others one of those parts?

Money and success give you the ability to do what makes you happy in life and to help others. The more people you help, the more successful you will become!

Success doesn't always come easy, but by working "Step-by-Step" and not giving up, success will come more quickly.

There have been many successful people who didn't become successful the first time around . . .

- Oprah Winfrey was fired by her first producer because she was "unfit for television".

- Bill Gates' first company failed.

- Walt Disney was told he wasn't creative.

- Milton Hershey had three candy companies that failed before he started "Hershey's".

- After his first movie role, Harrison Ford had an executive take him into his office to tell him he'd never succeed in the movie business.

- J. K. Rowling was a single mom living off welfare when she began writing the first "Harry Potter" novel. In 1995, all 12 major publishers rejected the "Harry Potter" script.

and the list could go on and on . . .

What I'm trying to tell you is –
write out your 15 Steps,
do them "Step-by-Step" and . . .

17
My Final Steps

"Step by Step and the thing is done".

Charles Atlas

I want to end this book with
something totally different
from other books -

I want you to help me achieve
MY goal . . .

My goal is to write a book that will help others achieve their goals through a 15 Step Process, comparing it to the making of a Peanut Butter & Jelly Sandwich.

I applied my 15 Steps to writing this book to help others and to give back. I'm almost there now, but . . .

I need YOUR help
with my
14th Step . . .

My 14th Step is to -

"Give to Children's Organizations through the sale of this book, so that they can help kids become successful adults".

Here's how it will work: For every book that I sell in print format, I will give a portion of the profit to children's organizations.

I will be choosing a different non-profit organization periodically, that specifically helps children in some way.

Children are our future! The type of adults they become will shape our world!

. . . so everyone who buys a printed copy of this book will help me have a successful 14th Step . . .

"Helping Children"

My 15ᵗʰ Step is to ⁃

Enjoy the fact that I made my dream come true ⁃ writing and publishing this book to help others achieve their goals, while helping children.

Hopefully this book will continue to sell for a long time. Together we will be helping children to live safe, healthy and happy lives, so that they grow up to enjoy their Peanut Butter & Jelly Sandwich "Stories"!

Remember when I talked about reaching out for help and assistance? Well that's what I just did with you!

Great luck with your Peanut Butter & Jelly Sandwich "Story"!

ABOUT THE AUTHOR

J. E. Edwards lives in Northeast Wisconsin and enjoys hanging around outdoors, especially near water, and loves watching how others make their peanut butter & jelly sandwiches!

In case you were wondering, the author's favorite peanut butter & jelly sandwich is crunchy peanut butter with grape jelly and crispy bacon on white bread - grilled.

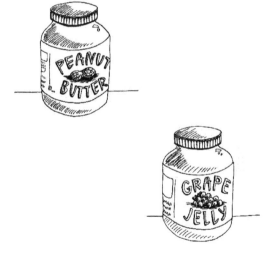

Made in the USA
Middletown, DE
04 October 2021